Viaggio

a journey through life

Colette Standish

Second Edition

All text and images
Copyright 2006/2020
Colette Standish

All rights reserved. No part of this book may be reproduced or utilized, , in whole or in part, including illustrations, in any form or by any means, electronic or mechanical, including print and electronic scanning, photocopying, recording, or by any information storage and retrieval system, without express written permission of the copyright holder.

ISBN 978-1-71651-618-4

Designed and Published by
Elf Magick Multimedia
Berkeley, California, USA

Dedicated to Mum

'Warm, dark low sounds. A nurturing keg slowly going round and round. Liquid matter solidifying into an abstract shape with eyes held together by an internal landscape of veins and blood. Another sound emerges faint but rhythmical and intense: surrounding: A heart beat.'

Smiling a seductive welcome, the Neon lights entice and tease you in. The wine flows thick and fast. Intoxicated and mesmerized, you are drawn in deeper and deeper. Unaware of the spell you are under, you search for that elusiveness that it holds yet never gives away.

Just when you think it's within your grasp a door closes behind you. Darkness. A clock ticks loudly. Before you know it you are running for your life. The first roar of the tide almost flushes you out, however, sober, tired and emotional you reach the crevice. Down below lava of liquid fire whips up a whirlpool as vast as the Milky Way. An abyss of endless beauty.

Calm with eyes open, you step over the edge and surrender to your fate.

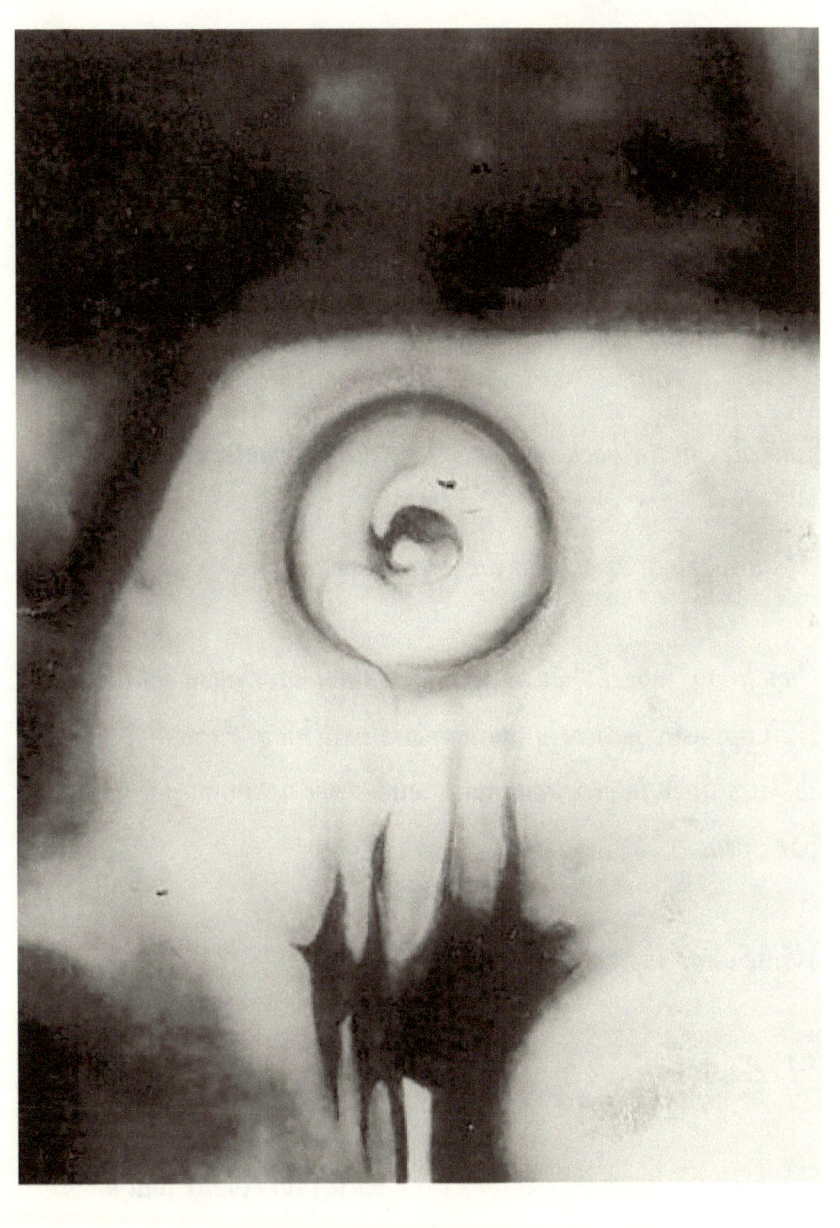

'Conversations in my head, loud, argumentative, agitated other times quiet, contemplative, subtle. Sometimes they want to be heard and verbalized, but most of the time they turn into shapes and colours and live in the back of my mind and only float to the surface when they ready to join the outside world.'

Landed, In the back of a taxi they start to materialize.

'It's important to stay in the present'

They know where they are going as they have often sat on the bench opposite patiently waiting and watching. Passing through the gates their interactions with others are acknowledge and the door opens.

White clear light.

A release.

'Verbalized the conversations turn back into colour and form transmitting the force of their internal landscape into the alien world'

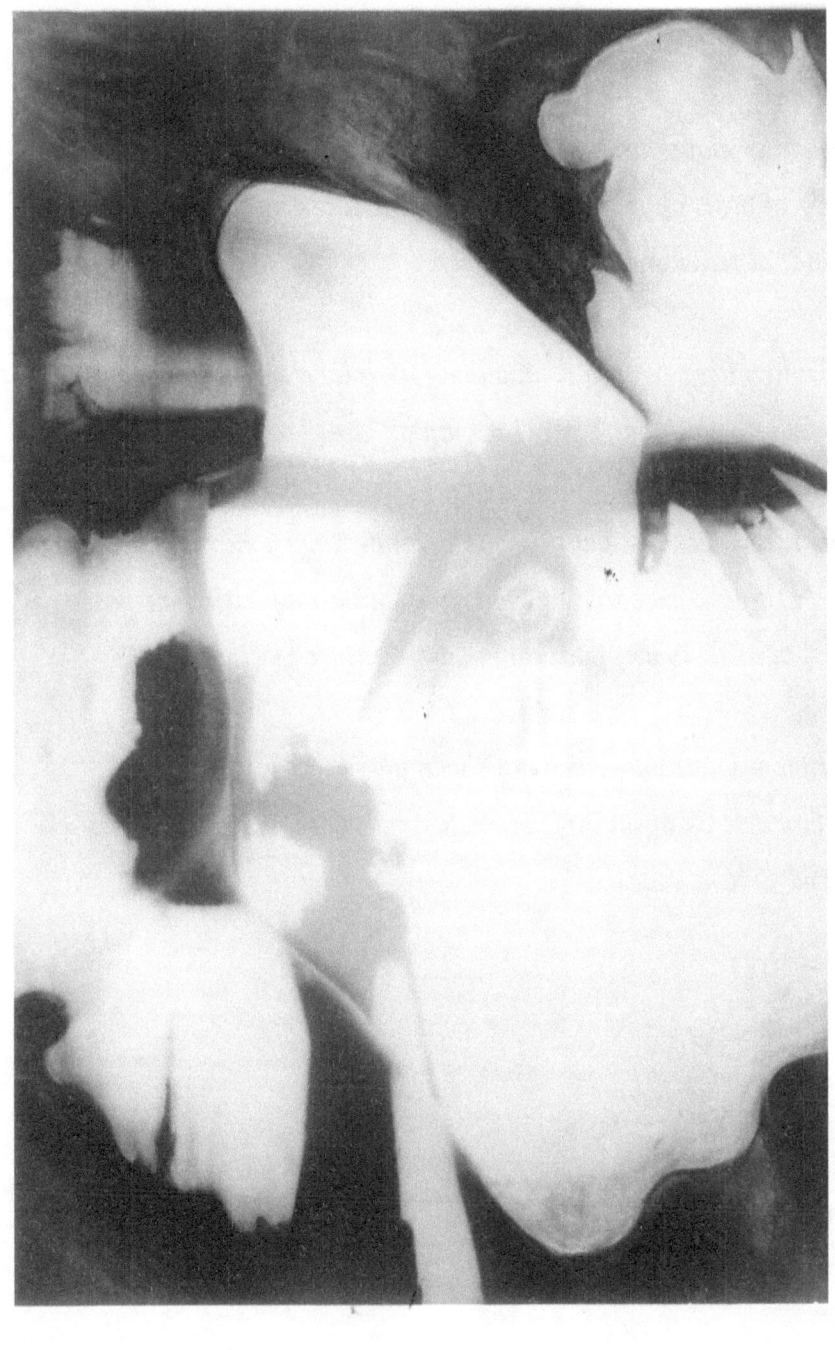

The shadow moves with me across the hostile landscape. In the distance an oasis of light and colour but here just me and the shadow that echoes my pale existence.

The shadow has been my companion for so long that it is difficult to imagine life with out it. Yet, I must. But hard as I try it will not leave my side. When I try to walk towards the colour and light, its blackness bars the way. Sometimes when its not looking I camouflage myself and try to fool it into letting me pass but it always finds me; flooding me with intense blackness

Sometime we dance together my shadow and I. A seductive tango that gels us or an invisible industrial noise makes are bones jitter and jerk.

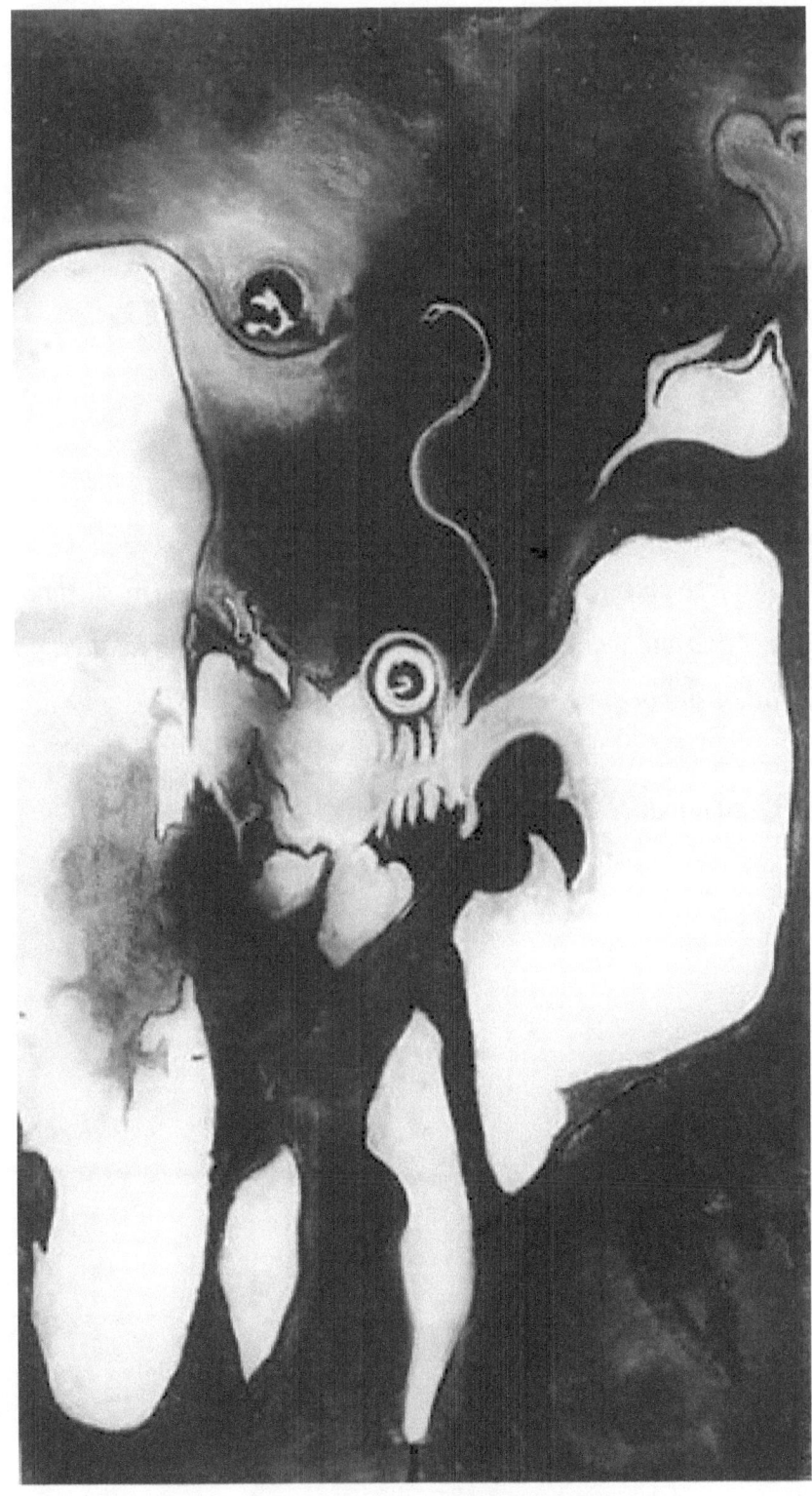

Most of the time we fight.
I get tired and weary too often.
Sensing this verge of submission, it throws itself on me manically lashing out till, worn out, I reluctantly put the metal jacket back on.

On the rare time that it sleeps, safe in it's blackness, my heart twitches and my eyes open. Once again colour and light appears. That place where love and harmony exist together. The shadow senses this and wakes. Its just a disturbed dream I reassure. Although not quite satisfied, it relaxes.

It's all a matter of time.

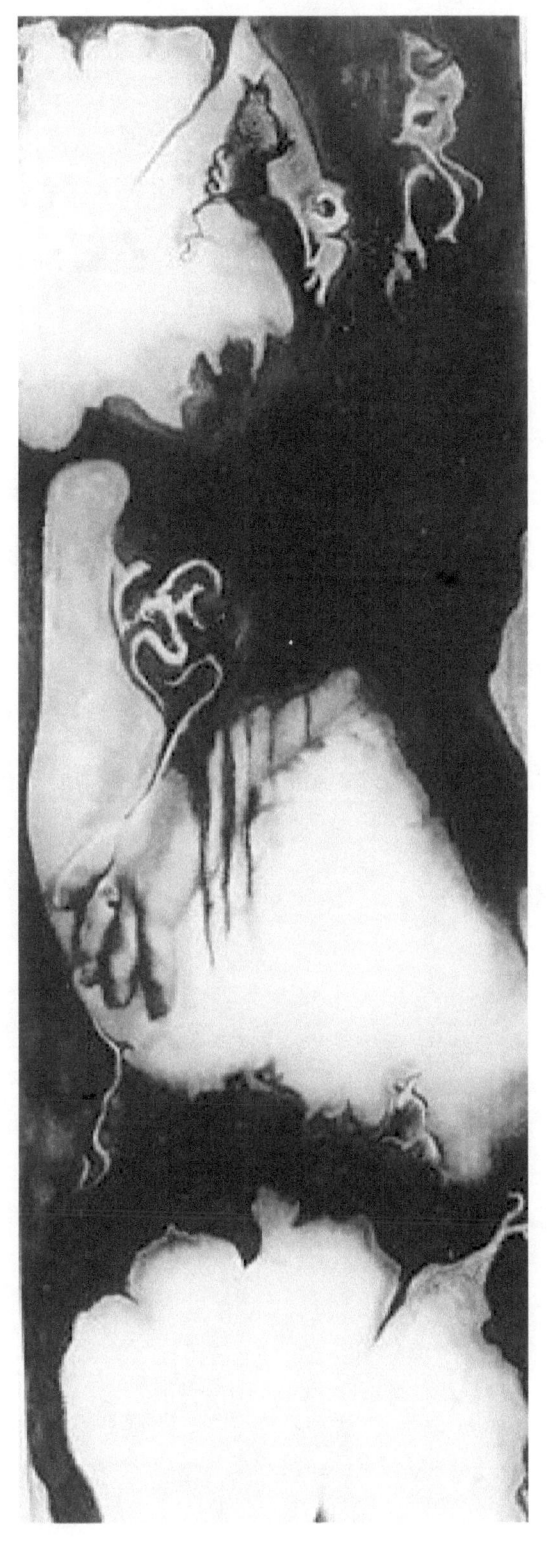

Going into a bar solo.

Get drunk to numb the feeling inside.

Cute + dangerous = A fuck in the middle of the night with a total stranger

Morning; Hung over, I creep out before he awakes.

Sick and lonely.

Not sure if it's a release or something to block the pain.

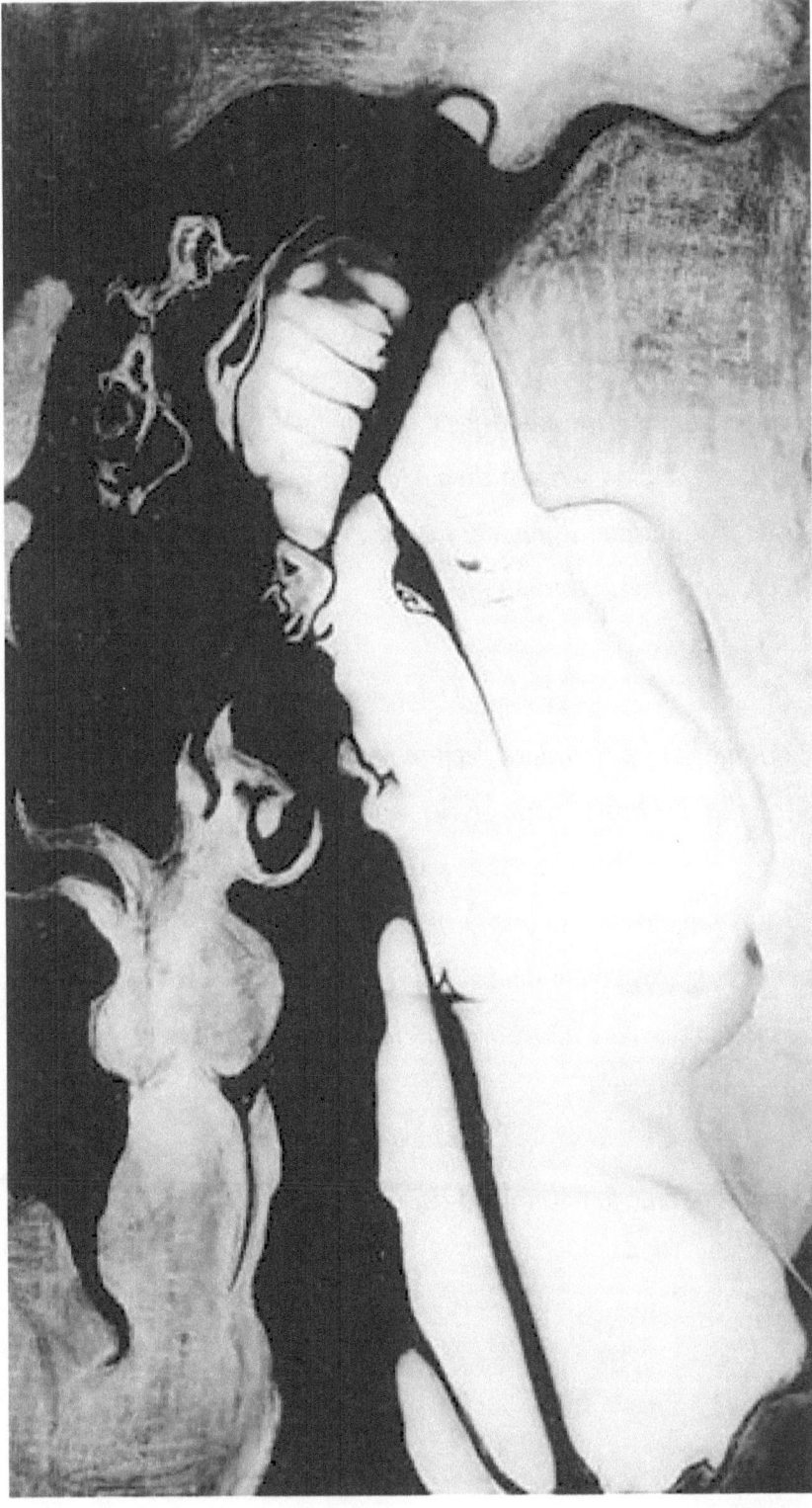

Tears burst forward flooding the senses. Tired and exhausted I try to swim against the tide but it only impacts and submerges me.

I am not sure of my feelings anymore. Is this relief from the pain or has the pain intensified? Are theses tears bitter or sweet? The pain soaring through my heart; is it life purifying me or is it poison killing me? All I know that it is tearing through my body leaving me numb. Is it warm or cold? I don't know.

A knife has been wedged deep in my heart. Movement only intensifies the hearts grip. Release is futile.

Is this knife trying to open my heart in order to let me feel again? Is this contaminated heart being cut open so that the toxins can dissolve into tears and leave my body making my heart clean again?

I won't be able to tell until the tears stop.

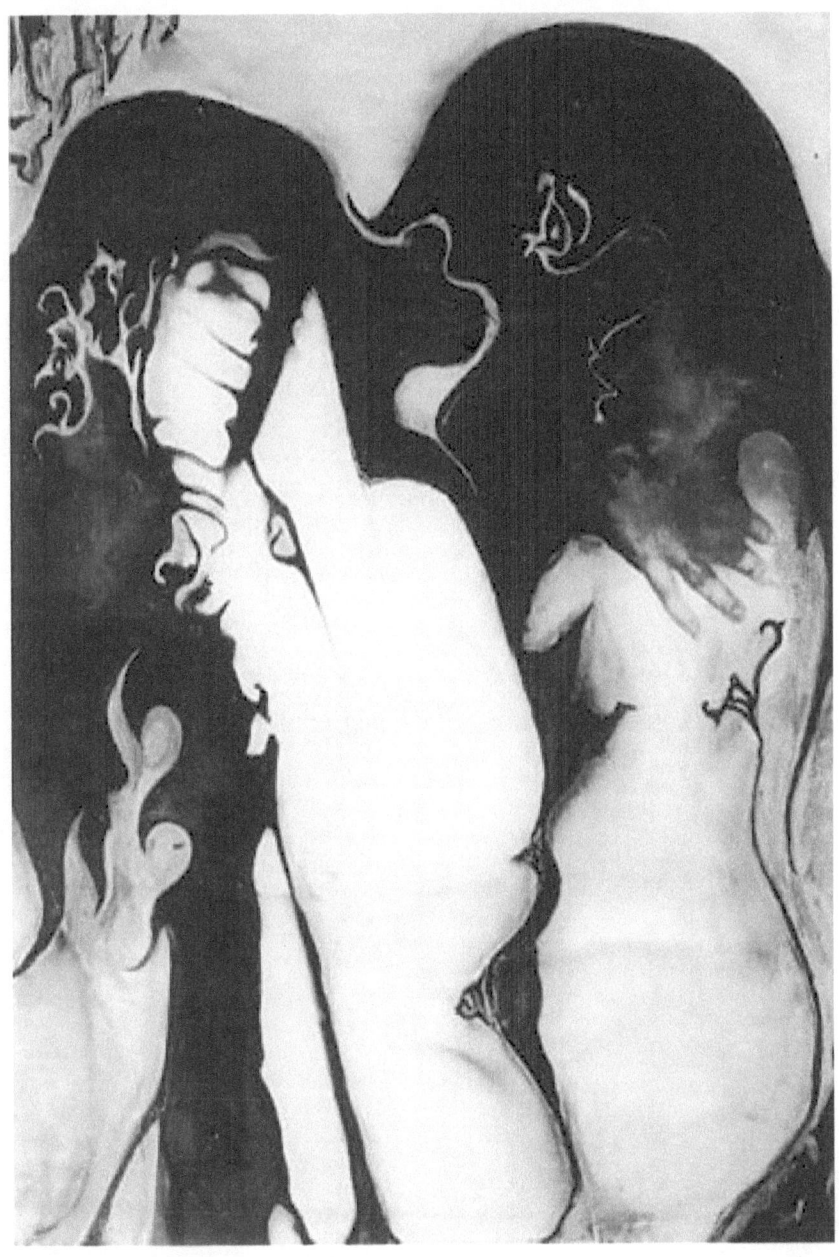

Nerves frayed

The future is a blur the past blind

Dealing with the present is all I can cope with.

Time flickers like a TV commercial.

2 mins and its gone!

All that's left is a negative. Black and white.

No Colour

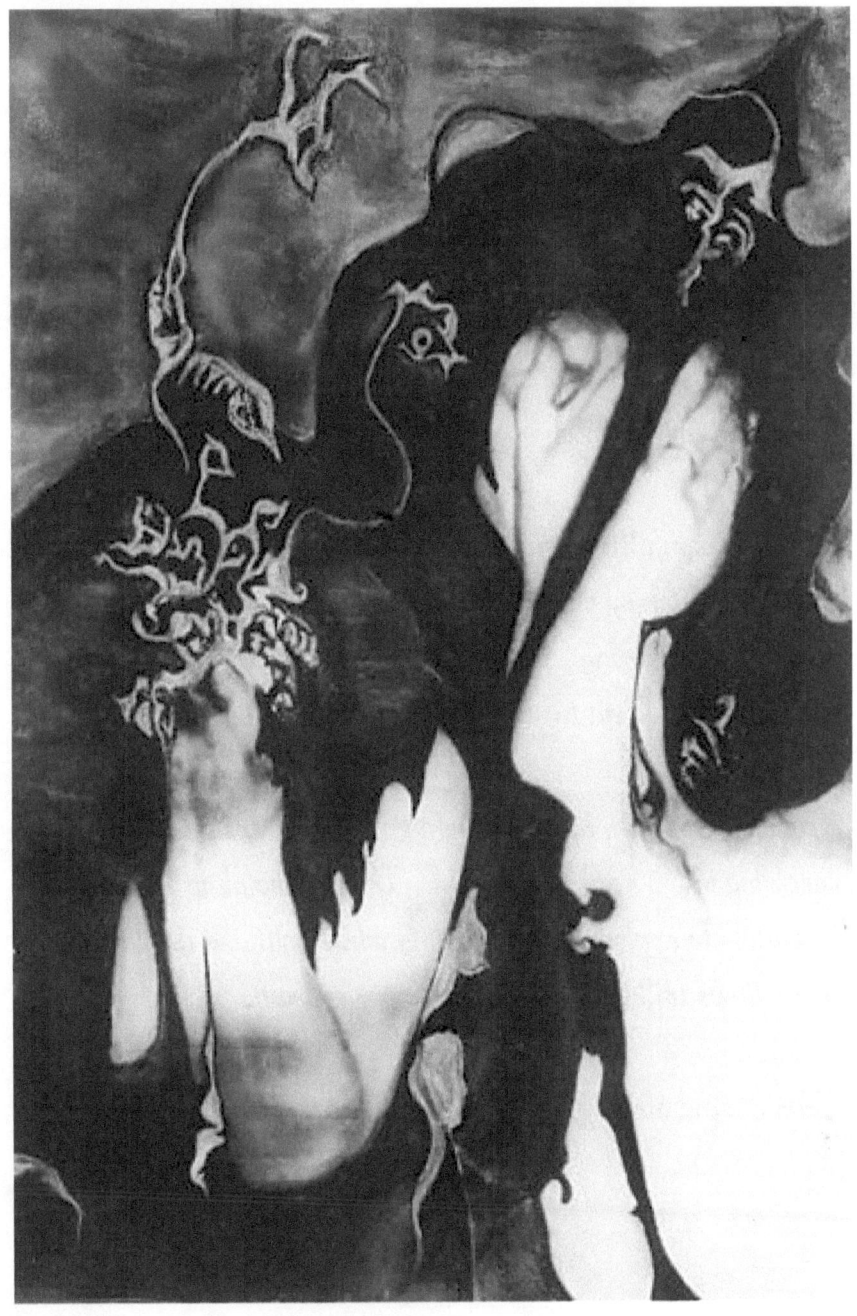

Everything is starting to malfunction. I can feel my body closing down. Panic and anxiety attack and my body starts to convulse. Unbalance and fragmented, all rational thoughts lie broken on the floor like shattered mirrors.

Gaunt and indifference.

Touch is painfully sensitive: burning coals or iced daggers. Clumsy, twitching and irritating. All smells repulse; no matter how subtle or strong. The smell of food, meant to be of comfort nauseates me. I eat to stay alive but for how long?

You exist but only in the twilight zone. You are on autopilot careering into a head on collision. The time bomb in your brain is waiting to explode into a blinding white light and the darkness that follows will race your body towards death.

Am I dead already?

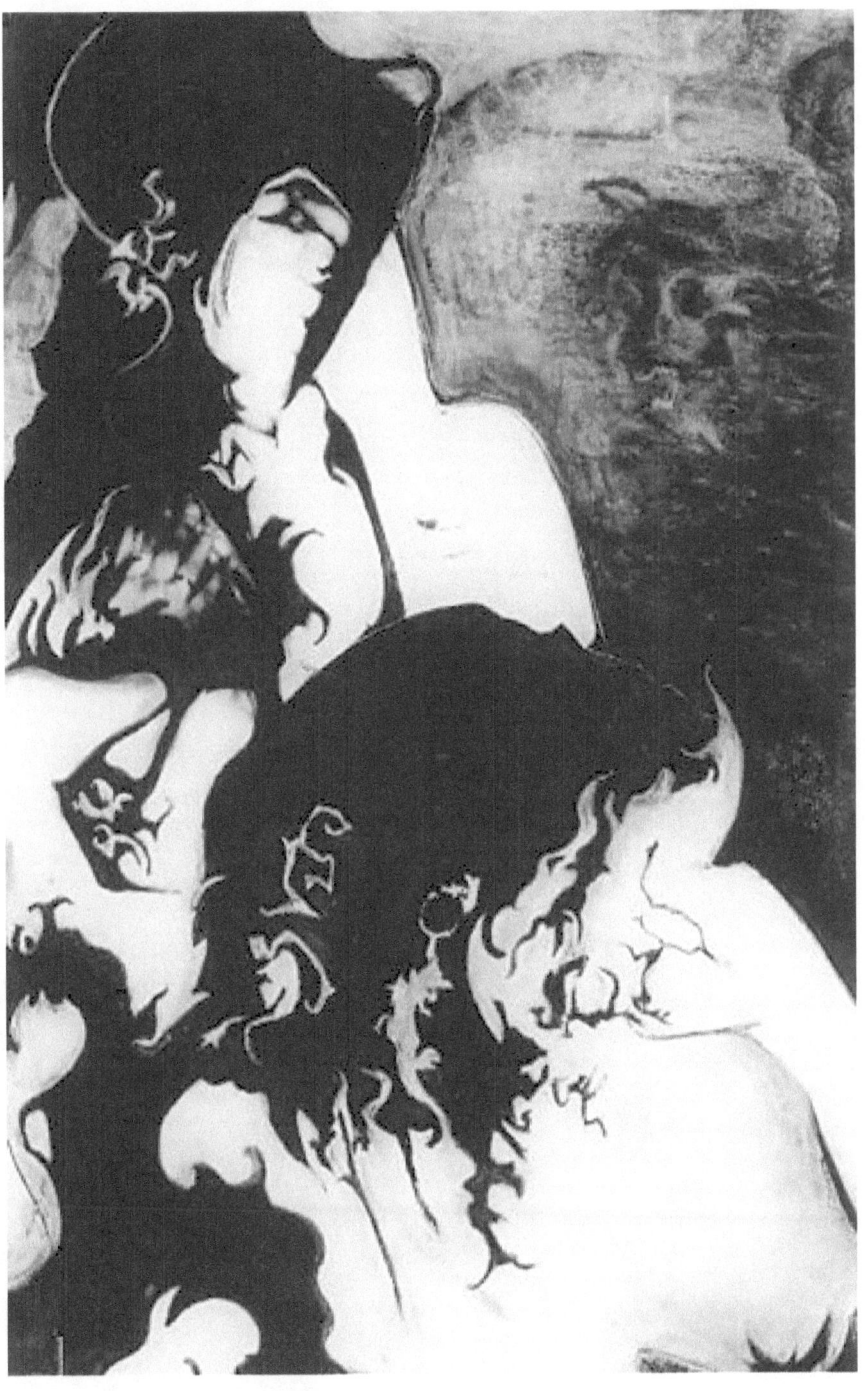

I wish I was

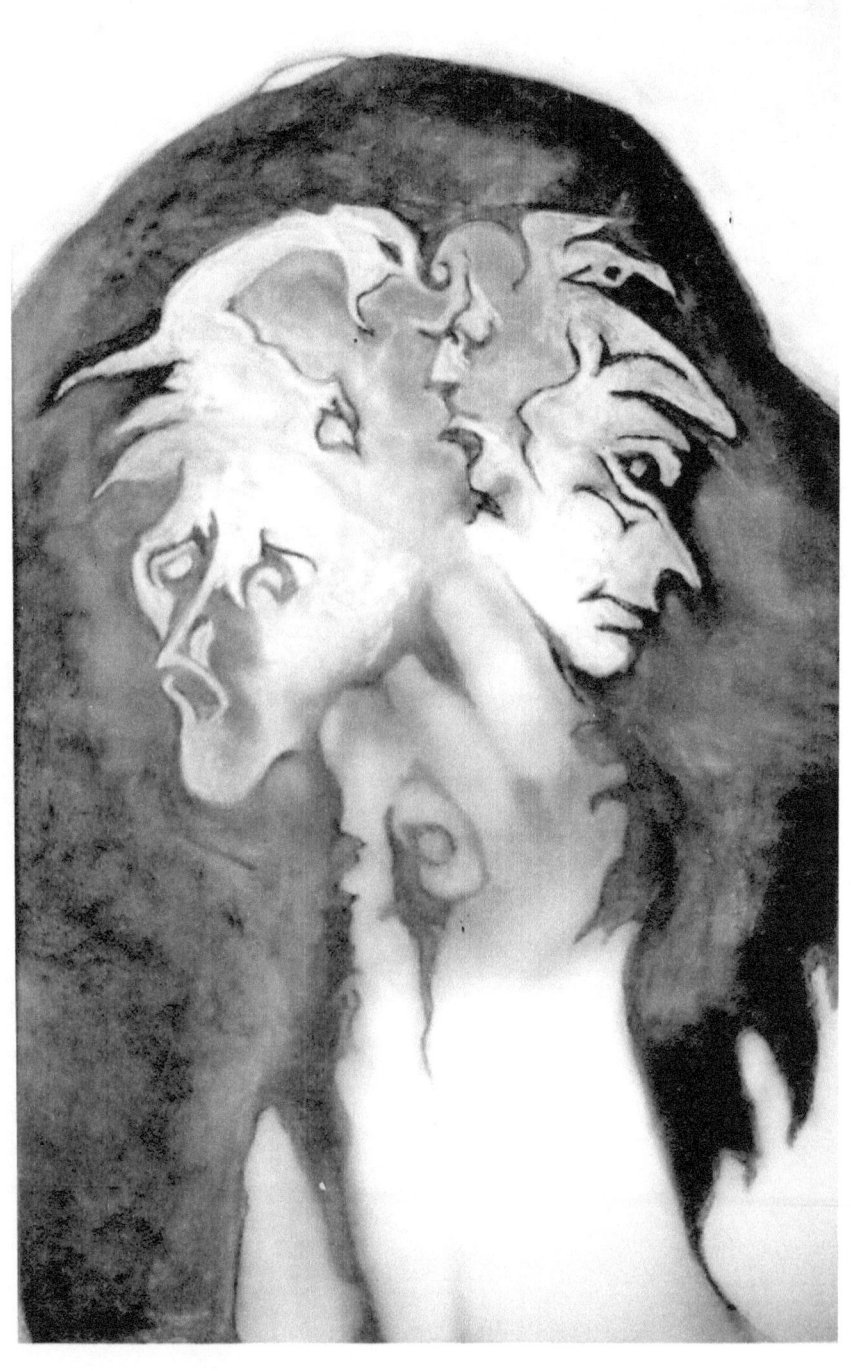

Cold.

Flat lined

Just before the light dissolves into the blackness forever it starts to flicker.

The last living thought as I leave this mortal coil is of hope and love.

The soul ascends overwhelmed with eternal love ready to start a new life

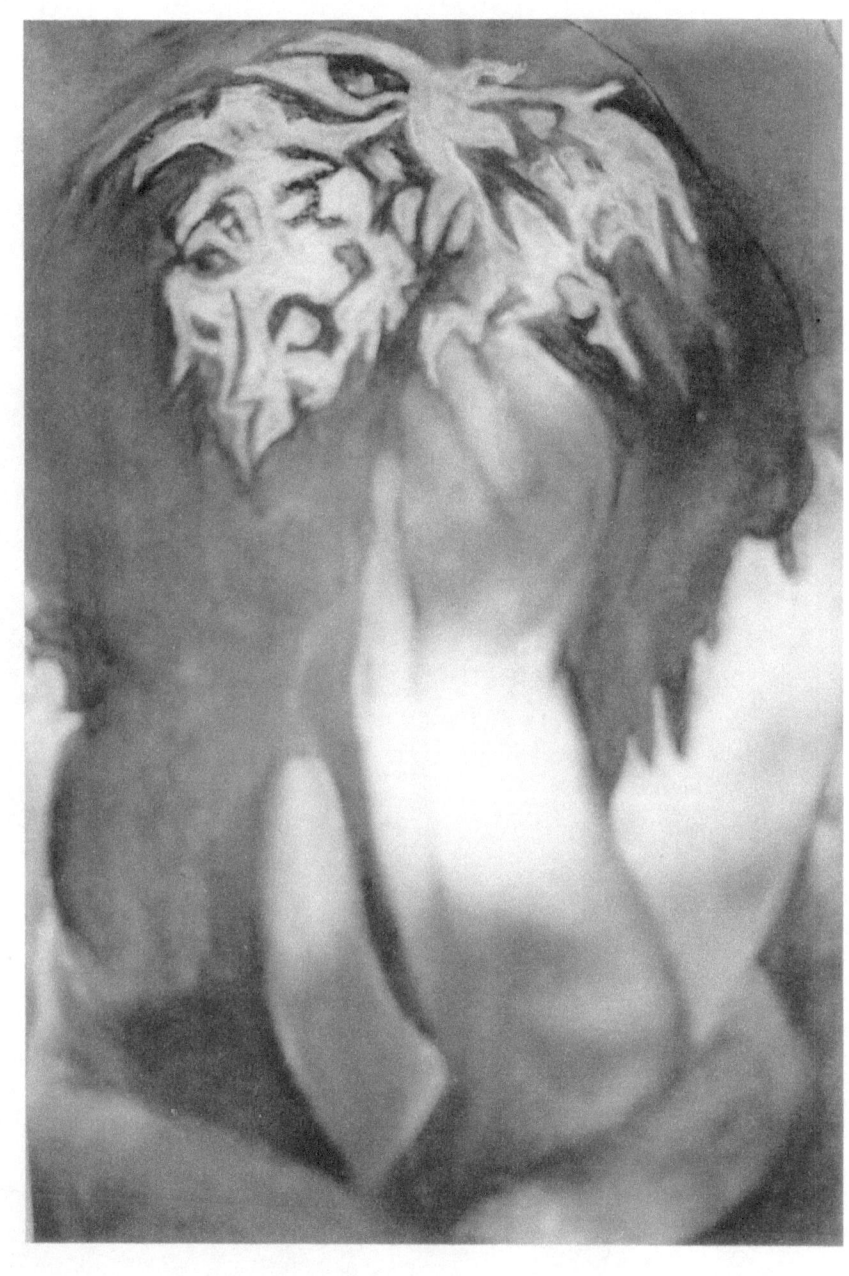

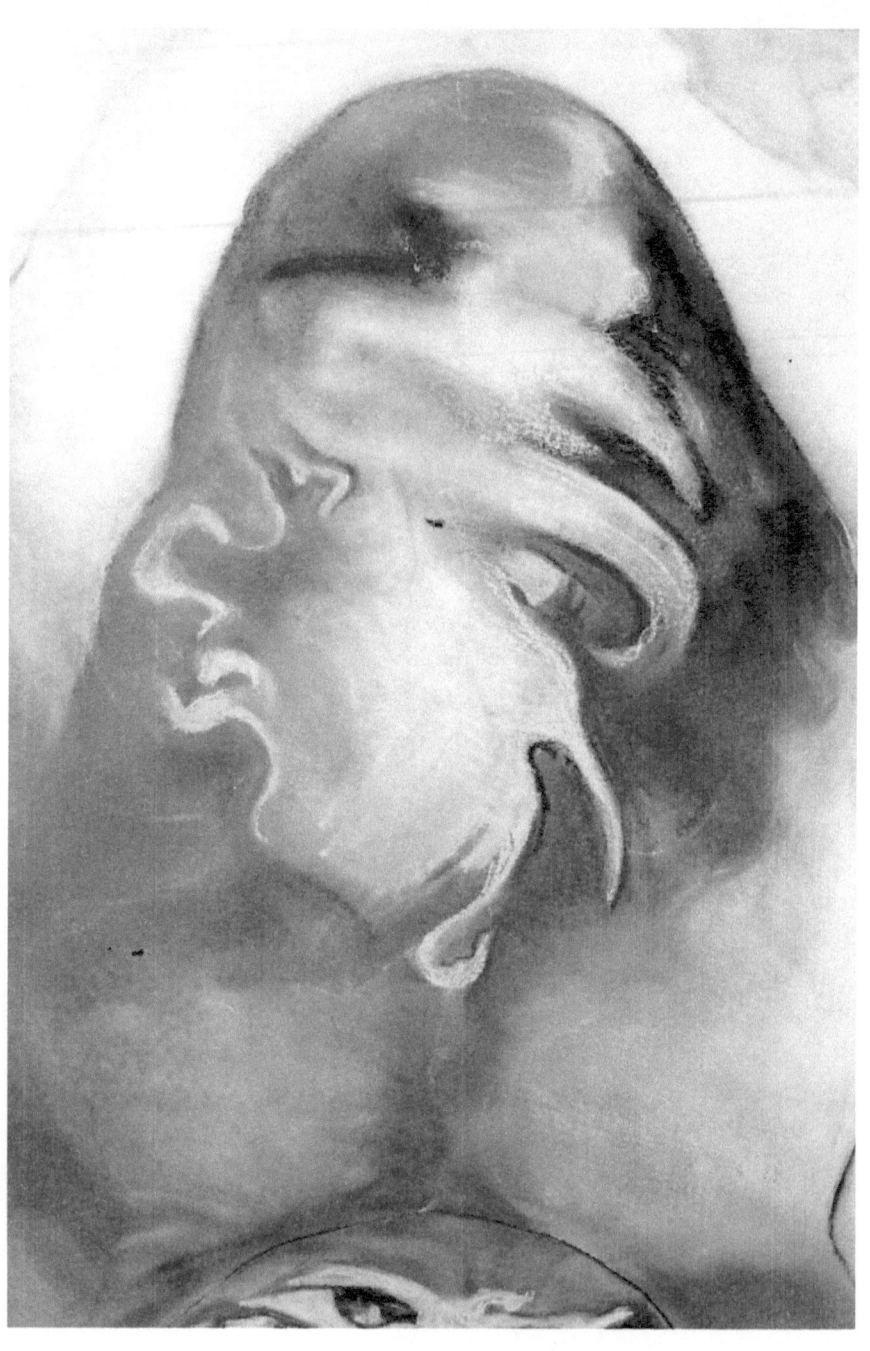

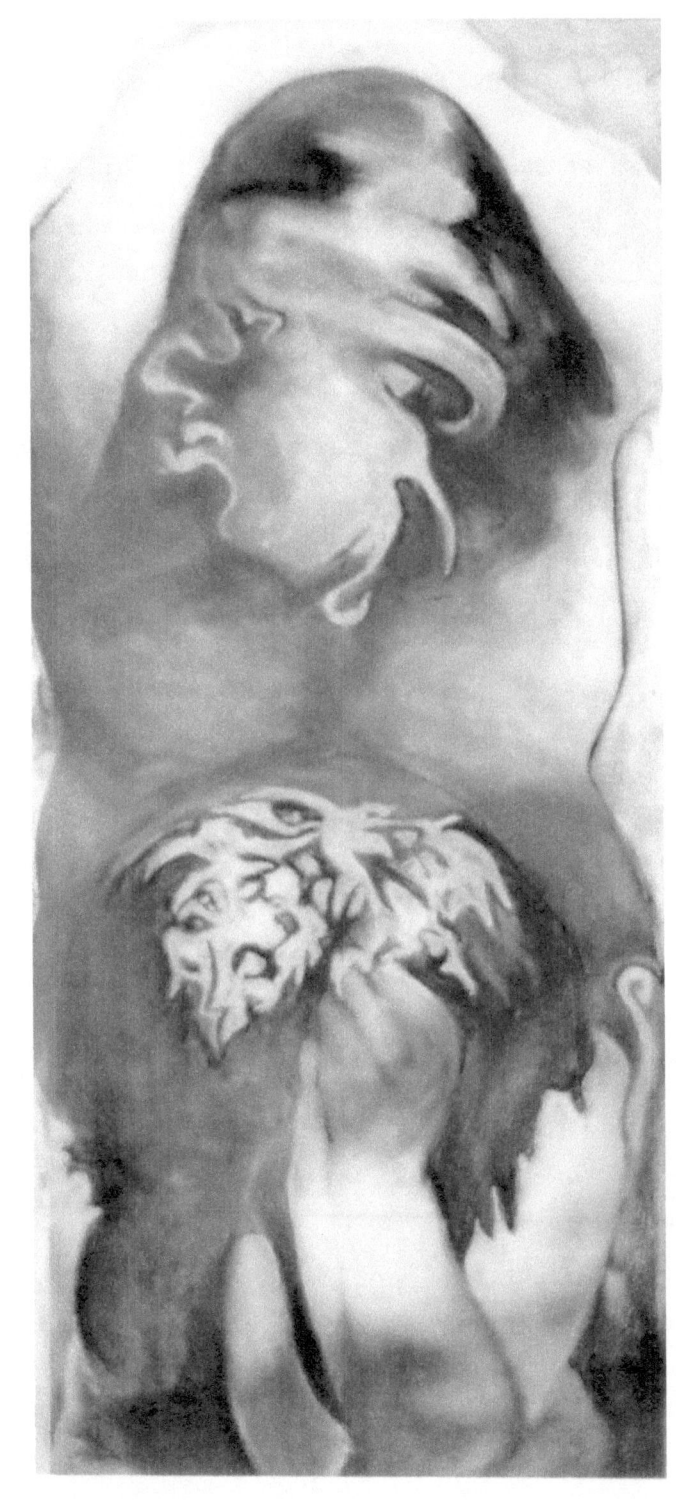

'Body and mind, air and matter, the ebb and the flow circulating each other, yet at the same time maintaining the existence of one and other.'

The physical body, heavy with matter and bone, wounded in pain. The mind reacts and injects an electric shock of relief. The mind burdened, pressure kicking against the brow, instinctively a hand soothes it with gentle strokes and kind words.

Equilibrium.

Synchronized, they resume their journey.

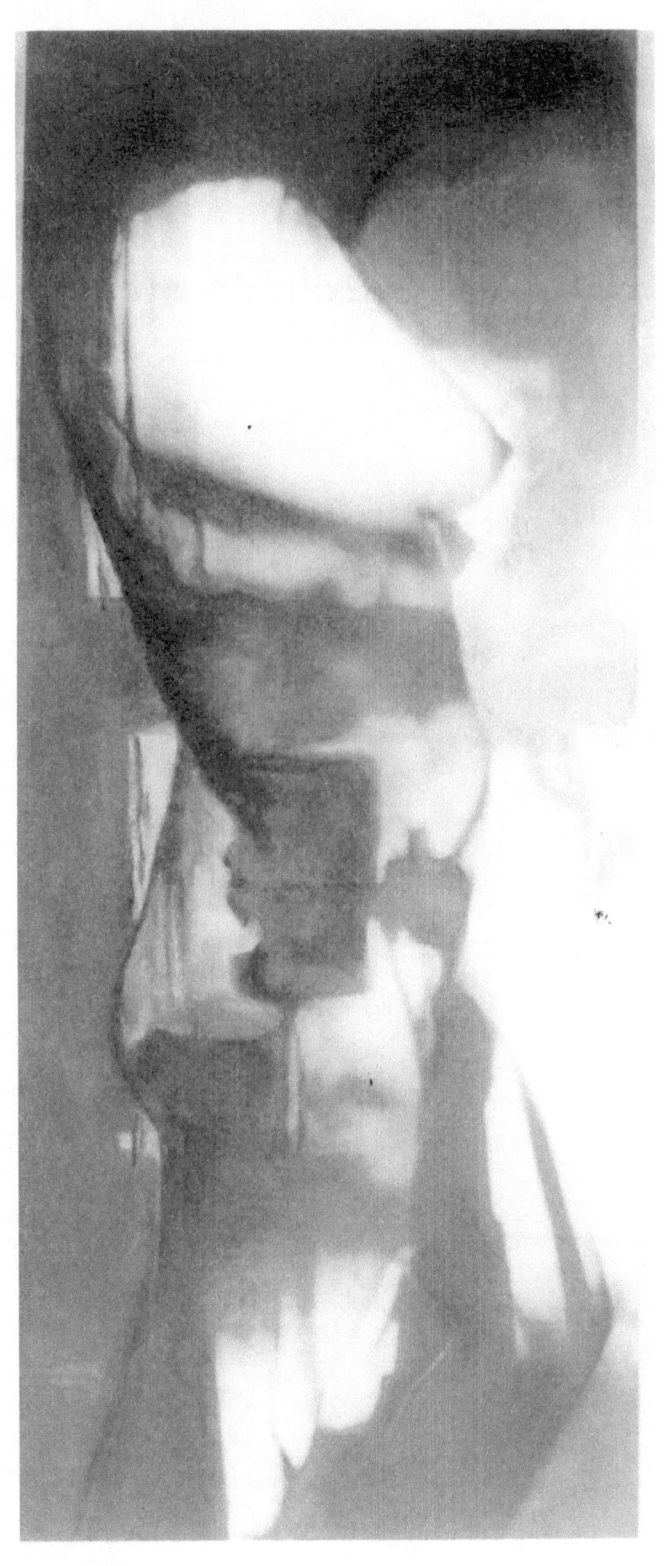

Could this be love?

I took a gamble, I opened my heart and throw it out there.

He caught it with both hands.

He could of run with it but he stayed and in return

Opened up to me.

I am shaken to the core.

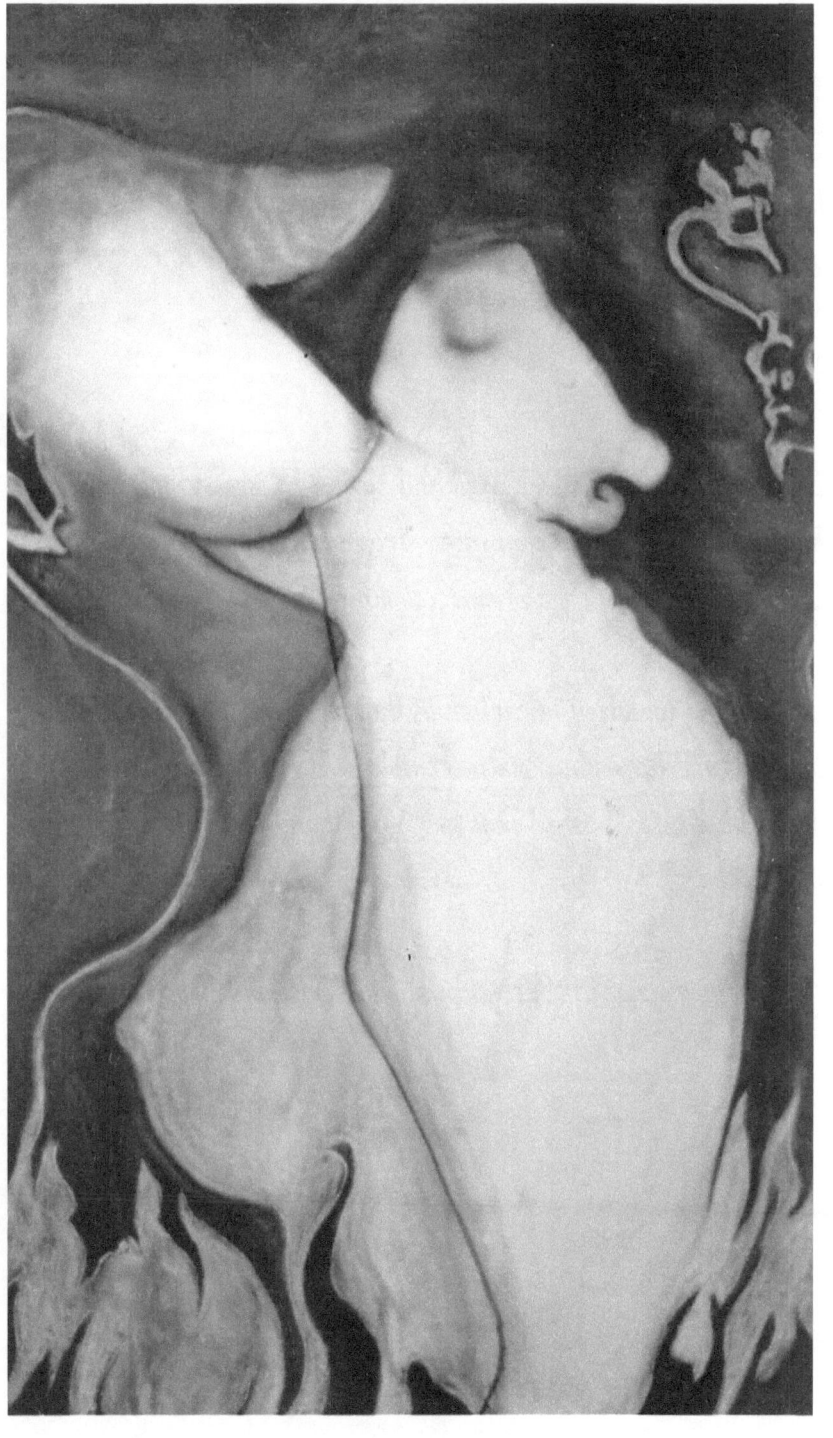

A screen separates us from the world. Even the ancient hieroglyphs that protect us turn their heads away; A sacred and private act of love

Kisses.

Kisses light and tender, hard and slow. Kisses to take my breath away I watch you move around my body tentatively. As you meet my eyes I can feel your confidence grow.

My mind wanders to earlier in the night dancing close and barefoot and how your body trembled. Trying to control your desires because I asked you to. Your hand on my thigh brings me back.

In a short space of time you have my past and present.

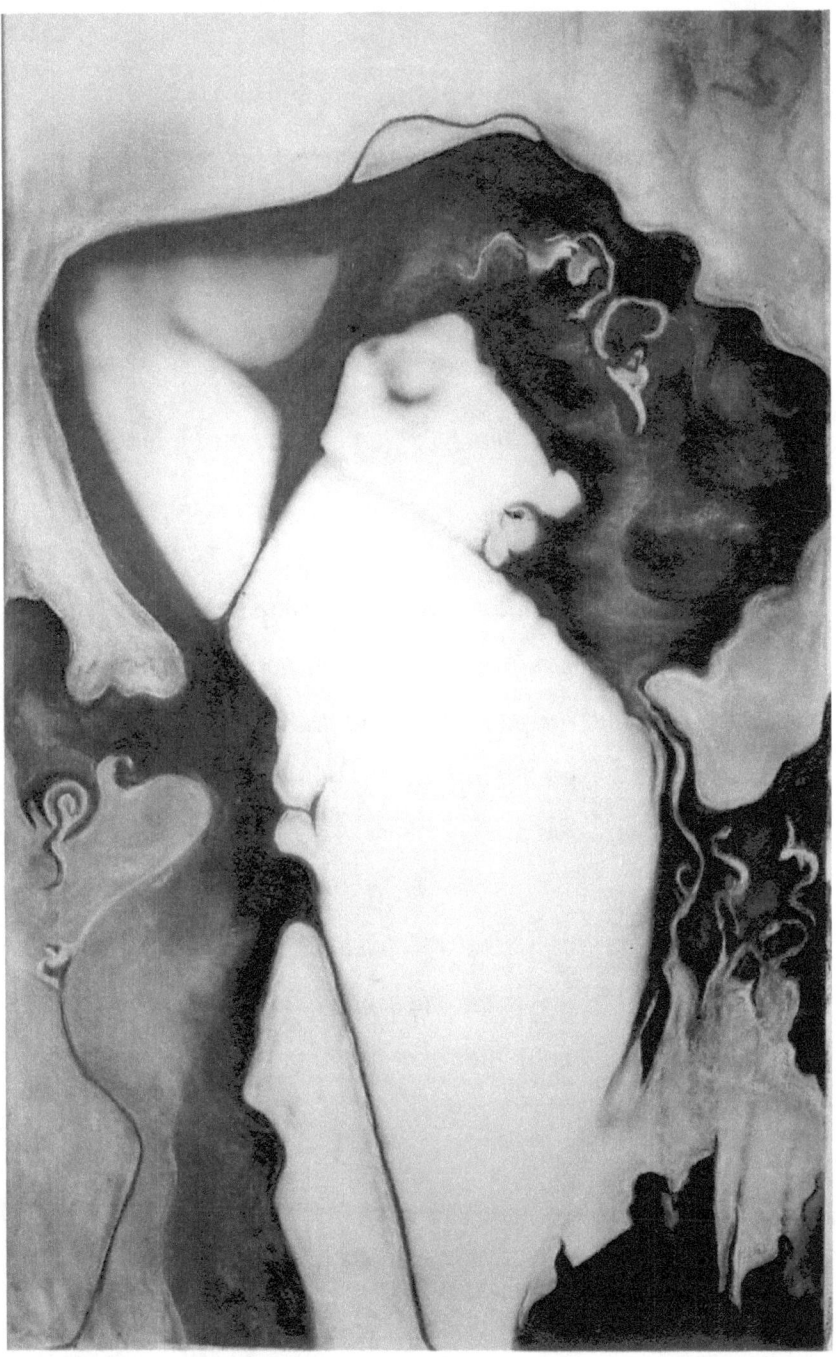

I watch you again. Your languid pose and the ease of your caress. Relaxed I responded sensually. No race. Your body pressed against me, your smell lingers on my breast and in between my legs.

Something in me moves which I thought had died a long time ago.

I touch you back. You have gained my confidence. A gentle smile hovers in between love and desire in your eyes. Your reaction is firm and the pain too full to bear. I pull away but you coax me back and dry my tears. Your hands on my face and hair reassure me I am safe.

My body arches, my senses overloaded. As I open up to you with your hands on my lower back you are there waiting for me. Waiting to explode your love straight to my heart.

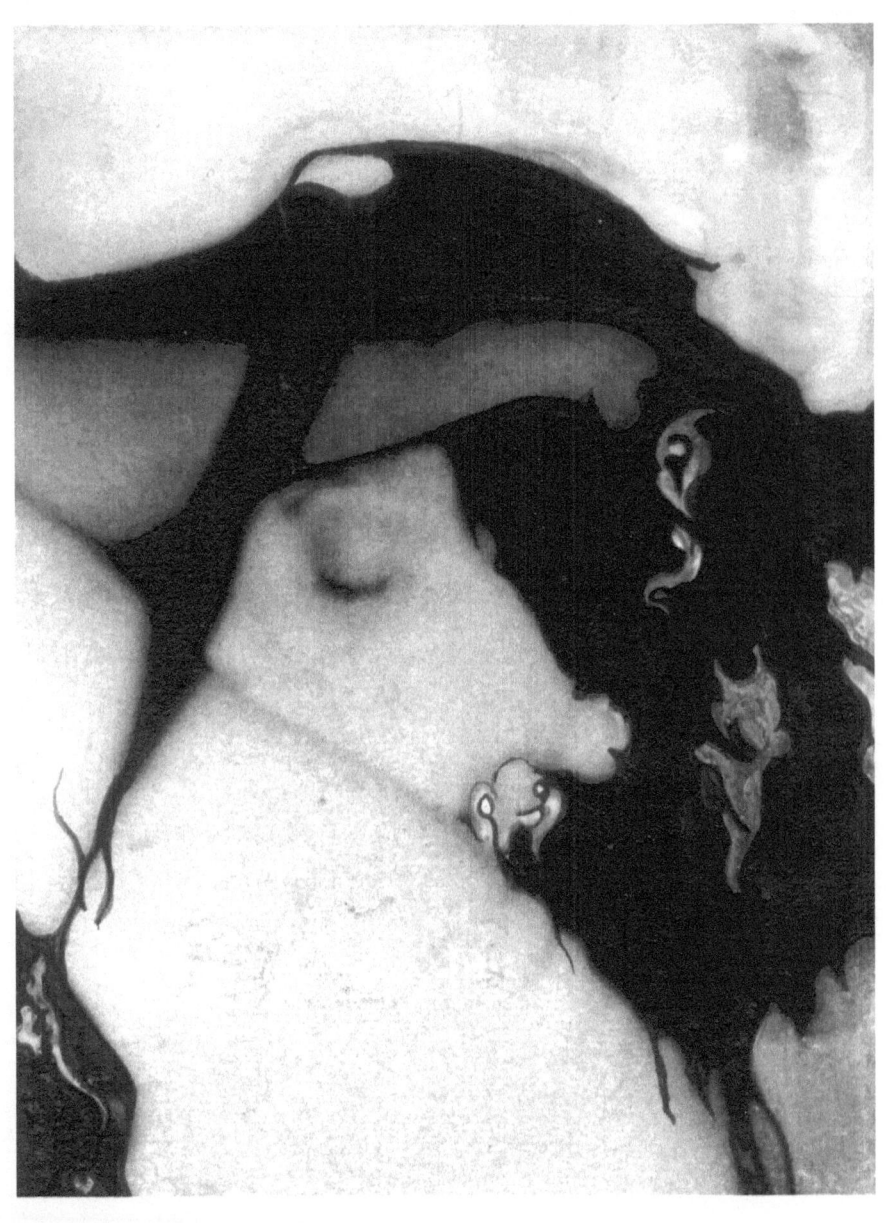

The heart is the boss and the brain second in command.

Decisions made by the heart are implemented by the brain which are then dispatched to both the left and right. The battle commences in the conference room where both sides mould, reshape, analyze and intellectualize and return to the heart for the final analyses. Back and forth from heart to brain. Be prepared to stay late. Decisions made, now is the time to negotiate with the millions of employees to make it all work.

'The heart pulses and vibrates rhythmically around this human machine, connecting and interacting with its many children. Nurturing and feeding its cycle of life.'

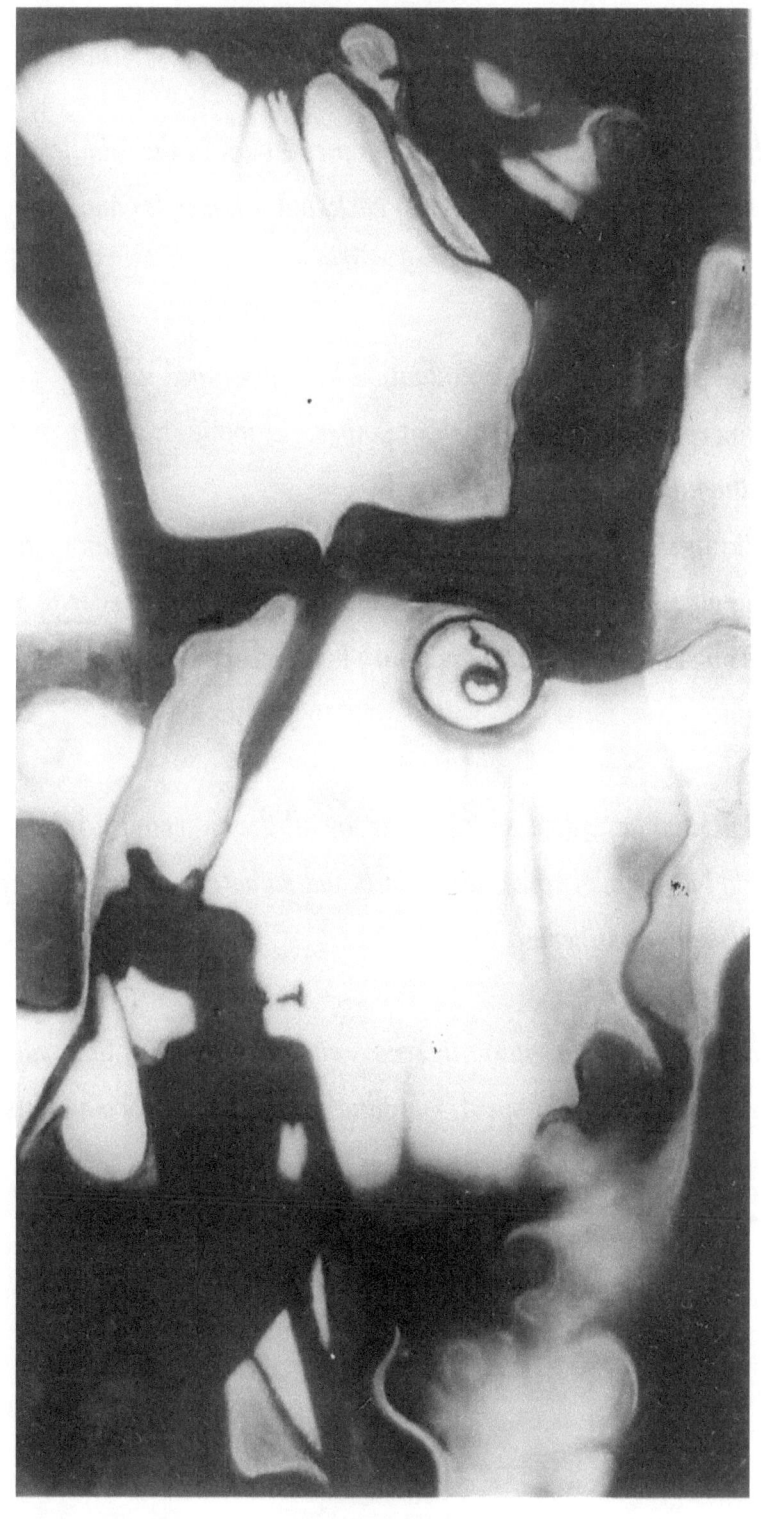

'The candles flicker and cut across me. I am in the middle of the cross. The cold steel arches my back and my nipples and hips jut out in reaction. I am quiet and still.'

Those first thoughts of intimidation have dissolved into empowerment. I feel a rush of power. I move, teasingly and feel the full force of female sexuality.
All my sisters are here with me; past and present supporting me urging me on. Confident, proud and full of female energy an orgasm starts to erupt through my body. I can take on the world!

Man may have died on the cross for all the sufferings of the world but woman comes alive on it and radiates. Female energy purifies mans suffering.

'The cold cross cuts into my senses and my eyes open to a naked woman stretched and spent. Glowing in the still flickering lights of female sexuality'

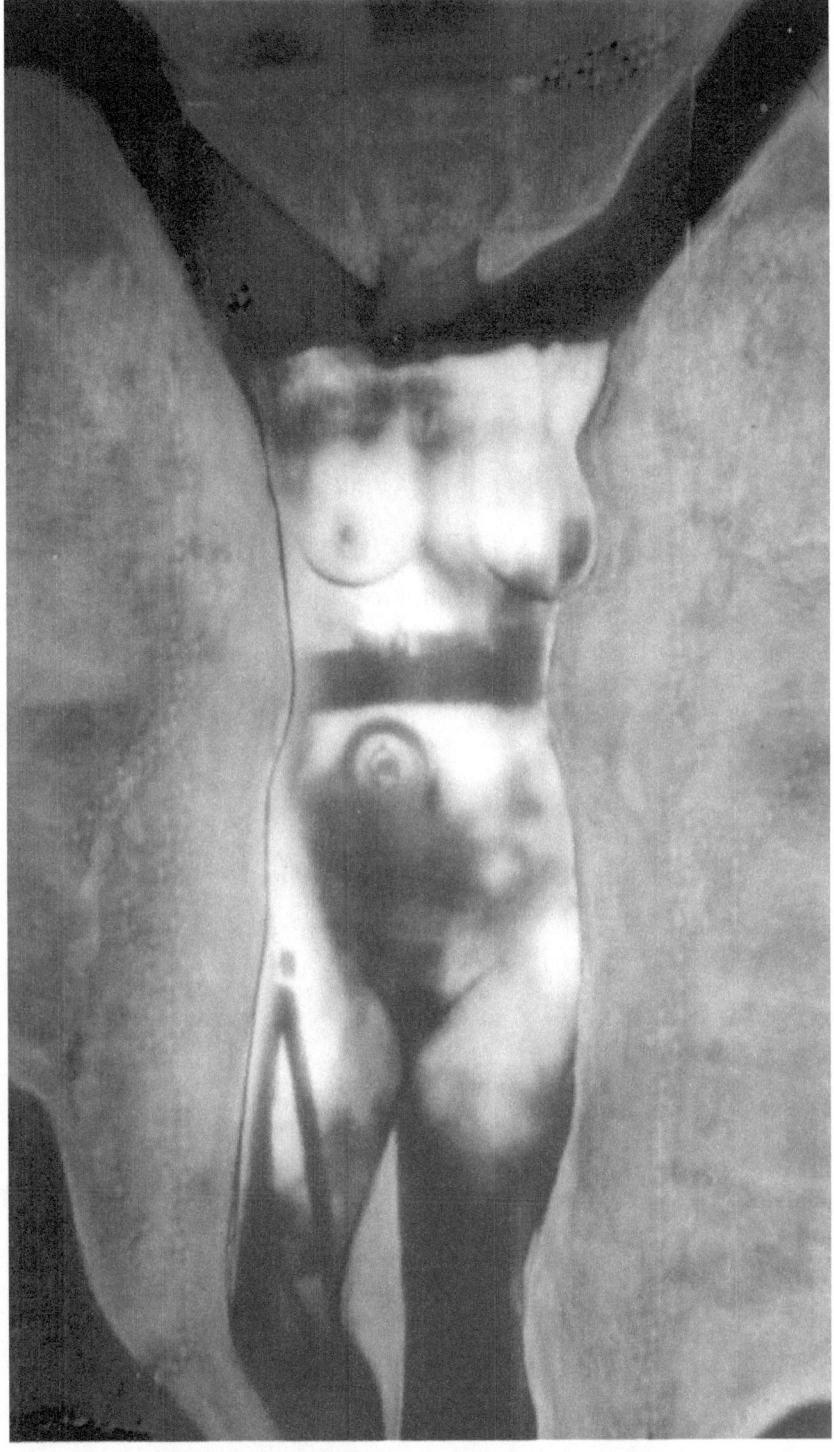

'10 years, 12 hour flight, one day respite, 3hr drive, jetlagged and exhausted, I know instinctively where I am'

The overcast sky gives a haunting look to the mountains, turning the pale green sage to silver. Behind the adobe wall lies a field of moss. A solitary white cross connects the field with the mountain. Silence so pregnated it's almost deafening. The wind plays soft sounds on the chimes nearby soothing me back from mediation. I become aware of another sound which is a lot closer; the slow beat of my heart. An awakening of sorts, too early to articulate but the sounds of those chimes will stay with me all my life.

'A long journey, my heart almost in pain beating against my chest wall. At last!! Home. Then quietness and a whisper: Peace

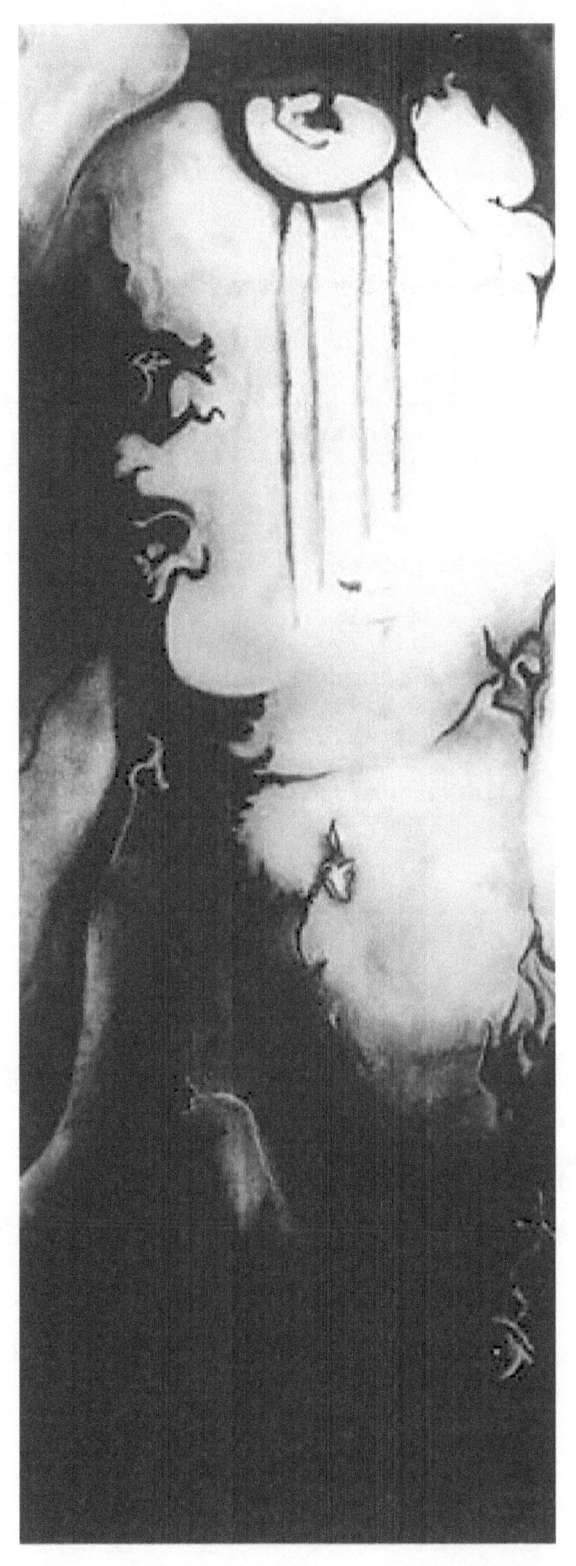

'The clouds have many different shapes, don't you think? Is that a cat? It looks like a cat! It certainly has a cat's tail.'

The sun and breeze playfully tickle my face. I sneeze.

'Put cream on your face or you will end up like your uncle', mum notes, 'too many days out in the sun.'

'Personally I prefer pale skin,' Nick joins us.

'Really? I prefer a bit of colour,' mum echoes.

'But you have red hair and freckles!'

'She's right Mrs. S, you would turn bright red like a lobster!!'

'Why you cheeky monkey! you are not too old for a telling off!'

'Well, you will have to catch me first'

Laughing, I watch the two of them chase each other across the big blue sky, waving as they go.

Life is good.

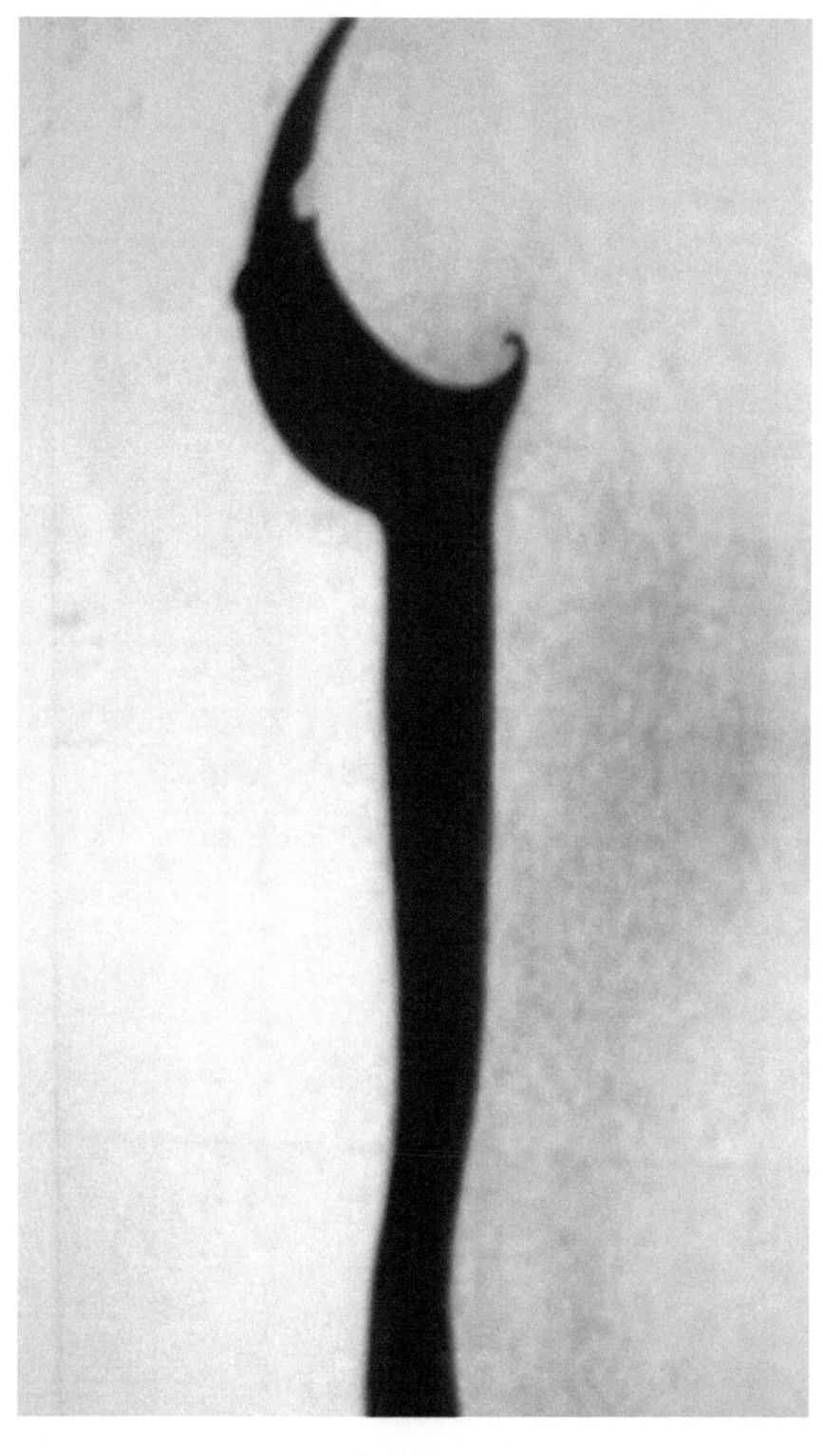

About the Artist

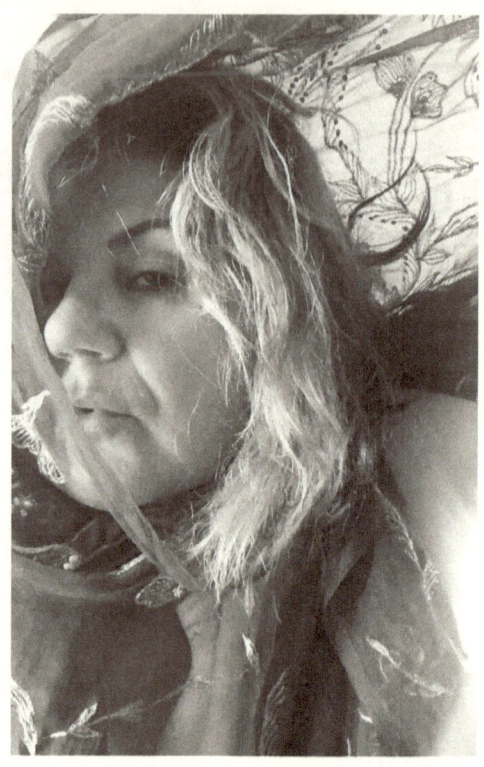

Colette Standish, is an English painter and photographer, and an independent scholar ngraduate from St. Martin's College in London. Her achievements include; Jessop's Photography Prize in London, 2000 and fellowship awards in New Mexico, Italy, and Spain. Her work is in many public and private collections, including the Museum of Fine Art in Santa Fe and the Anais Nin Foundation Art collection. Colette is a frequent contributor to, 'A Cafe in Space: Anais a Literary Journal ', and can be seen in Volumes, 8, 9, 13, 14 and 15. Colette's poem 'A Letter,' published in Volume 8, was made into a music video entitled, "I Was in Love… Still Am," by an Avant-garde collective EPI based in Manchester, UK and Florence, Italy. In 2019 was awarded a scholarship to study at the San Francisco Art Institute. Colette is currently based in San Francisco.

Colette Standish
fine art on permanent display

Pitminster Studios, Somerset, UK;
Anais Nin Foundation, Los Angele, CA;
Helene Wurlitzer Foundation, Taos, NM;
Museum of Santa Fe, Santa Fe, NM;

Private collections:

United Kingdom-
 London, Birmingham, Manchester, Oxford, Cambridge, Cardiff;

New Mexico, USA-
Santa Fe, Taos;

California, USA-
San Francisco, Los Angeles, San Diego

Other USA-
New York, Florida, Texas, Oregon;

Europe-
Austria, Sweden, Florence, Perugia;